C000003858

PHOTOGRAPHS FROM THE FIFTIES COLLECTION
'VARIETY ON THE SOUTHERN'
1948 - 1968

Compiled by Hugh Davies

© Noodle Books , Hugh Davies and the named photographers. 2011

ISBN 978-1-906419-58-5

First published in 2011 by Kevin Robertson under the **NOODLE BOOKS** imprint
PO Box 279, Corhampton, SOUTHAMPTON. SO32 3ZX

www.noodlebooks.co.uk

Printed in England by Information Press.

Front cover - FARNBOROUGH: S15 class 4-6-0 No. 30838 stands at one of the faces of the down side military platform at Farnborough with a return Air Show special for Basingstoke and stations to Southampton Terminus on Saturday, 8 September 1956. A close examination of the picture shows that Farnborough was working at maximum capacity with steam, disclosing that trains were ready to depart from both the up and down through platforms, as well as a fourth train (for the West of England) at the other face of the Military platform   Hugh Davies 94C

Frontispiece - WEST MOORS: M7 class 0-4-4T No. 30056 approaches the station at West Moors with a passenger train from Brockenhurst to Bournemouth West. In the background, Battle of Britain 4-6-2 No. 34051 'Winston Churchill' waits at the signal on the line from Salisbury with a short cattle train to follow the passenger service to Wimborne.   David Lawrence 5532B

Opposite page - ILFRACOMBE: Battle of Britain class pacific No. 34072 '257 Squadron' head-on at platform 2 at Ilfracombe on 7 November 1959.   Chris Gammell C1698

Rear cover - HAMWORTHY QUAY: This freight train, headed by B4 class 0-4-0T No. 30093, is standing on the site of Poole's first station, at the time (30 April 1957) then renamed Hamworthy Goods. Passenger services had ceased as far back as 1896, having survived the opening of the direct line from Bournemouth and the opening of the present-day Poole station by just three years, The service was a local working from Bournemouth via Hamworthy Junction.   Hugh Davies 235C

INTRODUCTION

The inspiration for this album came from an unlikely source, a discussion about commuting to work; specifically from Farnborough to Waterloo (and back).

From May 1953 to 1964, my regular train was the 7.37 am departure, which had originated at Southampton Terminus at 6.2 am (6.4 in the working book). It was formed of eight vehicles (with an extra Third on Mondays only) but it had a number of interesting characteristics. The consistency of the stock was not matched by the choice of motive power; on a number of occasions there were weeks when every day from Monday to Friday a different class of locomotive hauled our train; what is more, in a notable week in 1953 on four days we took different routes to Waterloo: direct up the main line; from Wimbledon via East Putney (fairly common); from West Byfleet (as it then was) via Virginia Water and Staines; and via Sturt Lane Junction, Frimley and Staines (for the latter, Sturt Lane box had to be open; fortunately it was switched in morning and evening rush hours for Woking - Frimley workings over the East curve). These diversions were normally unplanned and necessitated by 'incidents' on the main line such as the occasion when an unfitted freight split into two just under the canal aquaduct at Deepcut, between Sturt Lane East and Pirbright Junction.

During the winter, joining relatively late on the train's journey, one had the choice of having a seat (in which case you got on at the very end of the train) or being warm (in which case you stood at the front). The problem was that the stock had been left out in the open overnight with all the steam heating pipes left connected. It was also the train locomotive that came to move the stock into a platform at Southampton Terminus shortly before departure time. Thus with no provision for previous train heating and if the overnight temperature had dropped below freezing, the train had reached Vauxhall before steam had found its way to the last carriage. We passengers had a theory that some

locomotives managed to get the whole train warmed more quickly than others. Certainly on a memorable day when a T9 4-4-0 had taken over the train at Basingstoke we were particularly cold !

Our most common motive power was drawn from the ranks of the Remembrances (in their last years), Bulleid Pacifics, King Arthurs, Lord Nelsons, with occasional appearances from Schools and Moguls, HI5s and SI5s.

All this led on to a discussion on the variety in the railway scene as a whole, especially on the Southern and even as late as the 1960s. As I dug through our collection of pictures taken in those years, memories came flooding back. Thus this album is not a collection of classic three-quarter views of trains at speed. It is more a mixture of pictures intended to demonstrate the variety, and the unexpected, that could be found on the Southern in the first twenty years of nationalisation. I hope you enjoy them...

PADSTOW: Exmouth Junction allocated T9 class 4-4-0 No. 30729 shunting passenger stock at Padstow ready for the next departure for Okehampton via the North Cornwall line in July 1960. One other photographer intent also on recording the scene stood at the base of the starting signal.

Hugh Davies 441A

BODMIN NORTH: The Southern's tentacles reached into Bodmin - this is O2 class 0-4-4T No. 30200 at the buffer stops at Bodmin North whilst in process of running round its train, the 3.32 pm arrival from Wadebridge. This particular engine was continuously allocated to Wadebridge from at least August 1950 until March 1961.

Hugh Davies 33B

Right - MELDON QUARRY: The London & South Western, and later the Southern, obtained almost all its track ballast from its own quarries at Meldon, on the line west from Exeter. This is a view from the top of the quarry; an original Bulleid pacific about to pass in front of Meldon Quarry signal box with an up train. Not seen from here is that the windows of the signal box were protected by iron grills: a precaution against small pieces of stone flung out during blasting although on one occasion it was reported a larger piece of rock came crashing through the roof of the box. (The times of blasting were deliberately scheduled to avoid the times of passing passenger trains although freight workings might be temporarily delayed).

Hugh Davies 330A

Top - MELDON QUARRY: The remoteness of the quarry meant that many of those who worked here travelled to and from Meldon by train; a two-platform halt was provided and two services in each direction were scheduled to stop at shift change-over times. These were not advertised in the public timetables and those using the halt boarded and alighted from the first door of the first carriage of trains.

Hugh Davies 330C

WENFORD BRIDGE: The Wenford Bridge branch was best known as the home of the surviving three Beattie well tanks, and as the one china clay line that lay outside the Great Western's Cornish empire. However, here is evidence that it was not only china clay that was handled, with Wenford Bridge as a railhead that dealt with mixed freight and parcels for the local community. Witness then the goods office and the local collection and delivery lorry in 1958. ULY 517 is a Ford 'Thames'. Wenford Bridge was the furthest point from Waterloo on the Southern system.

Norman Simmons 2850C

DUNMERE: Beattie well tank No. 30587 crosses the road at Dunmere with the 10.0 am train from Wadebridge to Wenford Bridge in July 1960. There were no gates and the train came out of a cutting almost directly on to the road, which dropped down a steep hill on to the railway; the result was that once a day there was prolonged whistling followed by a good look-out!

Hugh Davies 529A

DUNMERE: Track maintenance at an ungated level crossing at Dunmere on the Wenford Bridge branch; Beattie well tank No. 30587 is waiting to proceed with the 10.0 am train from Wadebridge which, as usual, consists mainly of empty china clay wagons. It is Whitsun 1962.

Roger Holmes R391

HALWILL JUNCTION: Bulleid 4-6-2 No. 34081 '92 Squadron' arrives at Halwill Junction with the portion of the through 'Atlantic Coast Express' from Padstow; note the informative station nameboard on the right of the picture. The time would be around 10.55 am, a passenger joining at this station intending to travel to Waterloo due to arrive in London just after 3.30 pm.

David Lawrence 5626

Top - SIDMOUTH and EXMOUTH: Littleham station, between Exmouth and Budleigh Salterton; O2 class 0-4-4T No 30193 is crossing the departing passenger train. This member of the class was a long-standing resident of the shed at Exmouth Junction.

Chris Gammell C336

Right - SEATON JUNCTION and BRANCH: The triangular branch platform at Seaton Junction; M7 0-4-4T No 30045 has just arrived with a service from Seaton whilst King Arthur 4-6-0 No. 30452 'Sir Meliagrance' stands on the siding waiting to take a milk train from the nearby dairy.

Norman Simmons 2899A

PLYMOUTH FRIARY: These were the years when not only was there a variety of motive power but you never knew what you might be riding in; there was a common factor linking the Bisley tramway from Brookwood (depicted later), services between Clapham Junction and Kensington Olympia (also depicted later) and as here, the Plymouth to Callington workings. Here is a view of the latter: the 'gate set' at rest at the end of the line at Plymouth Friary, the Southern's base in the city.

David Lawrence 5262

EXETER CENTRAL: Up Southern trains from the West normally required a bit of help with the climb from Exeter St. Davids to Central; hence E1/R class 0-6-2T No. 32134 has just completed a banking job and is resting at Central waiting for a path back to St. Davids. This is a 1958 view, but by the following year only two of the class survived, and No. 32134 was not one of them. The design was a 1927 Maunsell rebuild of the Stroudley E1 class 0-6-0T with a radial trailing axle, larger bunker and new cab, specially intended for passenger services in the West country. Members of the class also found employment working out of Barnstaple Junction shed.

Norman Simmons 2897C

SEATON JUNCTION: Mums and babies cross the main line at Seaton Junction, with the porter keeping a wary eye on Adams 'Radial' No. 30583; in the distance an M7 0-4-4T is shunting milk tanks for the nearby dairy. No. 30583 is probably on its way back to Axminster for branch line duty following servicing at its home depot of Exmouth Junction

Norman Simmons 2840B

AXMINSTER: Bulleid 4-6-2 No. 34033 'Chard' heads a down train of mixed stock and livery arriving at Axminster; just visible on the left of the picture is an Adams 'Radial' 4-4-2T just running around its branch train for Lyme Regis. (See also next page.)

Norman Simmons 2417C

AXMINSTER: Adams 'Radial' 4-4-2T No. 30584 is ready to depart from the bay platform at Axminster with the single coach branch train for Lyme Regis, 21 April 1957.

Chris Gammell C346

AXMINSTER - LYME REGIS: A branch line with its 'own' class of locomotive not seen anywhere else. The three survivors of Adams' designed 0415 class 4-4-2T 'Radial' tanks were well suited to the branch. Here No. 30583 has just uncoupled from its train at Lyme Regis whilst holiday makers make for the exit and the sea. The presence of at least two coaches plus the fashions of the departing passengers indicate this was during the summer season.

David Lawrence 5122A

WAREHAM: BR Class 5 4-6-0 No. 73017 arrives at Wareham with an up service for Waterloo; alongside M7 class 0-4-4T No. 30129 has delivered connecting passengers from Swanage and Corfe Castle: at the time of writing these words, a sign of things to come (back)? A similar bay existed on the down side of the line.

Chris Gammell C2592

VERWOOD: U class 2-6-0 No. 31802 arriving at Verwood with a Bournemouth to Salisbury train on 6 July 1962; the signalman is on the platform ready to exchange tablets with the driver for the five-mile section to Fordingbridge which included the intermediate stop at Daggons Road. Just ahead of the board crossing is a 'Hallade Monument', a rectangular piece of concrete sunk into the ballast with a half a fishplate set into the top. (Further use of broken fishplates in the best tradition of railways re-use: set in concrete!). Its position marks the desired centre of the 'fourfoot', or sometimes a distance from the outside of the rail. (The theoretical mid point of the track, and not necessarily the actual mid point.) The ganger could check this monument, which had a small saw cut in the end of the fishplate, at the exact mid point of the track with his gauge, or a tape, and then realign the track to suit. They were used all over the Southern, probably from Exmouth concrete works, as they seem to have appeared during the Southern years. (The fact one is in place here is slightly unusual as there was already a fixed point: the platform, from which accurate measurements could be taken.   )

Chris Gammell C2302

DOWNTON: BR class 4 2-6-0 No. 76005 at the sole platform at Downton on the line from Salisbury to West Moors. In the background the signal box had been reduced to the status of a ground frame as far back as 1922 at which time the second platform was also taken out of use, all services now using the one platform. The train is bound for Bournemouth on 6 July 1962. All workings on this line were withdrawn just less than two years later, from 4 May 1964.

Chris Gammell C2307

NORTH CAMP: In the 1950s the railways still coped with large numbers of visitors to special events such as Farnborough Air Show; here Southern Mogul No. 31800 has taken over a train at Oxford, which originated on the Eastern Region (hence the Gresley stock) and is here arriving at North Camp from Reading. The loco will leave its stock here to be serviced and will go on to Guildford to be turned, watered and coaled. The date is 8 September 1957. The photographer recalls as a child seeing similar traffic at North Camp for the pre-war Military Tattoo at the Rushmoor Arena, Aldershot, when even the army relied heavily on the railways for delivering its display units to the show.

Hugh Davies 239A

FARNBOROUGH MAIN MILITARY PLATFORM: With the enthusiastic support of the Aldershot & District Traction Company, visitors to the annual Farnborough Air Show were encouraged to travel by train to Aldershot, changing there for a fleet of buses to the airfield. Whilst this was convenient for trains from Waterloo, it was not so easy for trains from elsewhere, so Farnborough Main was used by services from the west and by through trains from north of London. Here West Country 4-6-2 No. 34040 'Crewkerne' and U class 2-6-0 No. 31639 stand either side of the down military platform at Farnborough Main ready for departure the Bournemouth and West of England lines respectively. 8 September 1957.

Hugh Davies 239C

FARNBOROUGH MAIN: Learning the road - venerable former LSWR inspection saloon DS1 is propelled past Farnborough by an unidentified T9 class 4-4-0. What had commenced its life as a director's saloon in 1885 had undergone considerable rebuilding over the years including being mounted on a shortened underframe. The roof mounted gas tanks, used for the kitchen appliances, were removed in 1958.

Bob Barnard 8119

FARNBOROUGH MAIN: M7 class 0-4-4T No. 30246 approaching Farnborough with a down local freight working from Woking to Basingstoke.

Bob Barnard 8053

FRIMLEY JUNCTION and the STURT LANE East and West curves.

In the 1950s and into the 1960s there survived a set of junctions just east of Farnborough on the LSWR main line linking with the Ascot to Ash Vale line which passed underneath the main route at this point. The two junctions were named Sturt Lane East and Sturt Lane West, both controlled by one signal box at the mid-point on the down side of the line; the junctions with the Ascot line were controlled by Frimley Junction box which was also responsible for issuing and collecting the tablets for the single-line stretch to Ash Vale (which remains single to this day). I deliberately refer to the survival of these junctions for there had been no regular service over the west curve (Frimley - Farnborough Main) for many years; although the east curve (Frimley - Brookwood) had three services in each direction in weekday rush-hours into the electrified era. It was for this reason that the local lines only were electrified west of Pirbright Junction and a sub-station was located at Sturt Lane. Despite their scant use, both curves were double–track to the end, maintained as a strategic facility.

Top - West Country Pacific, No. 34012 'Launceston' negotiates the West curve at Sturt Lane with a return Farnborough Air Show excursion to the Midlands. As referred to above, this curve was not electrified, but the cabling carried the supply to Frimley Junction from the sub-station, just out of sight on the right of the picture.

Bob Barnard 8270

Bottom - A pair of 2-6-0s, the pilot being No. 31798, bring the empty stock of the 'Farnborough Flyer' air show special up the West curve at Sturt Lane on to the main line; the coaches had spent the day at Ascot for cleaning; the locomotives will return to their home shed of Guildford via Woking. Sturt Lane signal box is just visible to the right of the lead locomotive.

Bob Barnard 8208

FRIMLEY JUNCTION: BR Class 4 2-6-0 No 76016 heading a Harwich to Aldershot troop special passing Frimley Junction signal box and heading for the single line to Ash Vale.

Bob Barnard 8294

Left - CAMBERLEY: A link with the past, Adams 0395 class 0-6-0 No. 30580 at Camberley with the local pick-up goods. This archaic survivor from an earlier era spent some time at Guildford in the 1950s finally being withdrawn in 1957.

Bob Barnard 8063

Above - In Ascot Race Week 1955, the peace of the station is shattered as West Country pacific, No. 34033 'Chard' passes through Camberley with a return excursion to Salisbury. This train will, after passing Frimley station, take the west curve at Frimley Junction to join the main West of England line at Sturt Lane West and so reach its destination.

Bob Barnard 8272

READING SOUTH: U class 2-6-0 No. 31630 standing next to the Railway Clearing House Office near Reading South shed; this office was a lively place in pre-nationalisation days. Note also the Huntley and Palmers' biscuit factory on the right of the picture. This firm had its own railway system with fireless steam locomotives and generated a lot of traffic by rail.

Norman Simmons N645B

READING SOUTH: The London end of the down main platform at Reading General was an excellent vantage point to watch the activities at Reading South. On Easter Monday, 11 April 1955, an SR 2-6-0 indulges in a spot of shunting.

Norman Simmons N291C

READING SOUTH: G6 class 0-6-0T No. 30160 is working hard shunting freight stock in the goods yard at Reading South on St. George's day, 1955.

Norman Simmons N646A

READING SOUTH: The signal box at Reading South, 23 April 1955. Note that the box had all-round visibility, the line rising from right to left behind the box is the 'new' junction between the Southern and Western Regions added in WW2 as an aid to trains transferring between the GWR and SR. Another wartime feature being the bricked in windows of the locking room. In addition to the old junction for through running, there was also a low level connection, latterly used mainly for freight transfer and passing via a tunnel under the WR main line: hence this was a busy box. With the aforementioned all-round vision there was no provision for a 'facility' for the signalman on the operating floor, hence the wooden privy under the steps. Notice also the box appeared to benefit from two stoves.

Norman Simmons N254D

WINDSOR: The Southern's terminus at Windsor is called Riverside and, appropriately, it is seen here adorned with directions to Salters' Steamers in 1954. The station also possessed a Royal waiting room, as did the Western's Windsor Central station.

Brian Connell B11/1

ASCOT: Into the 1960s Ascot still had two full-time signal boxes. This is the interior of 'B' box with Stationmaster Powell and Signalman Bowditch demonstrating the working to visitors, who include some from the WR S & T Department.

Mike Walshaw 6801

GUILDFORD to REDHILL: During the reign of Dr. Beeching there were real fears that the non-electrified SECR route from Wokingham to Reigate might disappear: such thoughts now seem almost unbelievable, given the line's resurgence. However, many of the more rural stations have lost their facilities, typical of which is Gomshall, here seen awaiting the arrival of a train for Redhill on 22 February 1954. Sadly all the station buildings seen have gone, except for the WW2 signalbox (no longer serving any purpose, for Gomshall is now just plain track).

Norman Simmons N174D

CHALKPIT LANE CROSSING: During the years covered by this album, a widespread activity was the delivery of drinking water to some of the more isolated crossing houses and signal boxes. Here Q class 0-6-0 No. 30539 is performing such a function at Chalkpit Lane Crossing, near Betchworth, between Dorking and Reigate. Sometimes it was a job for the guard, although on this occasion the fireman is carrying out the duty: perhaps it is hot water that is needed? The date is 22 February 1955.

Norman Simmons N173F

Left - TONGHAM: Until 1952 there was a direct route from Guildford to Farnham; it left the SECR Reading line at Ash Junction and possessed a local passenger service until 1937. The most important intermediate station was at Tongham, seen here on Christmas Eve 1960, exactly one week before complete closure of the line took place on New Year's Eve.

The view is looking through the station towards Farnham, the section past this point having been taken out of use in 1952. Tongham station predated the opening of a station at nearby Aldershot; this meant that the building of the extensive Military Camp was served by Tongham, together with North Camp station on the SECR. In later years Tongham provided connections with the gasworks system which had its own locomotives. In the early years of the route, some services worked this way right through from Guildford to Bordon, Alton and even on to Gosport.

David Lawrence 4674

Bottom right - NORTH CAMP: One of Bulleid's delightfully ugly Q1 class 0–6–0s has arrived at North Camp with a pick-up freight; the goods shed is still in use, and the gasworks (out of sight) is still functioning. The picture was taken from a Reading to Redhill train with, behind the photographer, an oil depot and the island platform. The location is today just plain track, but when the picture was taken on 23 April 1955, the signalbox by the level crossing was kept busy 24 hours a day. The box eventually closed on 7 May 1980.

Norman Simmons N254E

Top - GUILDFORD: The turntable and a half-roundhouse provided the locomotive facility at Guildford. Whenever the turntable was out of action, locomotives that could not be catered for on the shed sidings were sent out to Shalford, the first station on the Redhill line. The site of Guildford shed is now a multi-story car park.

Norman Simmons N544E

LONGPARISH BRANCH: T9 class 4-4-0 No. 30284 standing at the platform at Longparish, then the limit of the line that once formed a connection from Hurstbourne to Fullerton. The service was the 8.45 am freight from Andover Junction and will shortly be ready for the return trip to the junction at Fullerton. 9 July 1955.

Brian Connell B42/7

FULLERTON JUNCTION: Busy times at Fullerton Junction; on the left is T9 class 4-4-0 No. 30310 with the late running 6.40 am Eastleigh to Andover Junction freight; on the right is another T9, No. 30284, shunting the Longparish branch freight (the 8.45 am from Andover Junction), 9 July 1955.

Brian Connell B42/6

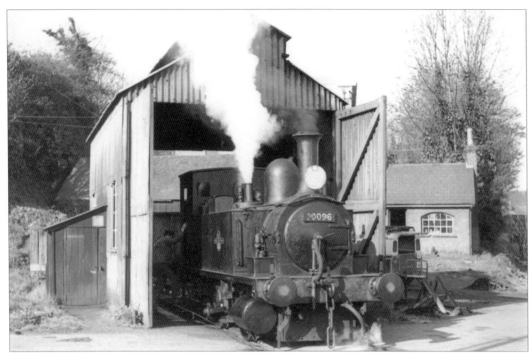

WINCHESTER: At first sight this looks as if it could be a branch terminus, but in fact it is the shed at Winchester with its normal occupant, a B4 class 0-4-0T, enjoying the sunshine. The shed was situated on the down side of the main line, just north of the station and the loco was employed on local shunting duties including, on occasions, attaching and removing tail traffic.

Roger Holmes R0680

ALTON: On a cold winter's day in 1954, pull-push set No. 662 stands at Alton forming the next departure for the Meon Valley line; the platform destination finger board describes the train as being for 'Fareham, change for Portsmouth'. Intending passengers for the latter having to travel via Cosham as the line between Fareham and Gosport (and thence via the harbour ferry) had closed to passengers in 1953.

Brian Connell B20/7

ALTON: 700 class 0-6-0 No. 30698 shunting in Alton yard at 11.50 am, 17 April 1957. The engine had recently arrived from what was then the truncated remains of the Meon Valley line at Farringdon. After finishing its business here, its next port of call will be at Medstead at 1.45 pm.

Mike Walshaw 6419

CHAPEL CROSSING: Class B4 0-4-0T No. 30082 on a morning down transfer goods at Chapel Crossing, Southampton, probably from the nearby Northam Yard, 25 June 1956.

Mike Walshaw 6312

BENTLEY and the BORDON BRANCH: This is a 1957 view of the branch train for Bordon in the bay platform at Bentley, in charge is M7 class 0404T No. 30027. The concrete pillar nearest the camera was the start of a fence separating the down main platform from the branch. A gate was provided to cope with the number of troops changing trains, especially at weekends, on their way from and returning to camp at Longmoor.

Norman Simmons 2382B

KINGSLEY HALT: The train just seen at Bentley has now reached Kingsley Halt, the only intermediate stopping place on the branch to connecting with the Longmoor Military Railway at Bordon. This rather bleak platform was afforded some limited degree of weather protection by rows of Poplar trees planted either side of the line.

Norman Simmons 2383A

RINGWOOD: M7 class 0-4-4T No 30108 at the platform whilst propelling the 2.30 pm from Bournemouth West to Brockenhurst on 18 May 1963.

Chris Gammell C2751

Above - BISHOPS WALTHAM: No. 30033 at the freight only station at Bishops Waltham, 8 March 1958. Despite losing its passenger service as far back as 1933, freight continued to be handled until 30 April 1962, the majority of this business, certainly in the latter years, being coal: witness the stacks on the ground alongside the engine. Opened in the 1860s as a private company, the branch was soon absorbed into the LSWR network and whilst grandiose plans for an extension beyond Bishops Waltham to Brockbridge and even Petersfield were made, these came to nought. Today the station site has been obliterated by road improvements with one road, the B3035, taking for the first part of its course, the route where the engine is standing.

Chris Gammell C695

Right - BOTLEY: The same engine at Botley, the junction of the branch with the Eastleigh to Fareham line. To the right is the former branch platform, the actual point of divergence is just beyond the brake van of the train. Ironically a short stub of the branch still survives today and is used as a shunting spur for roadstone trains arriving from the Mendip quarries.

Chris Gammell C692

HAYLING ISLAND: Possibly immortalised in the name of a local pub, 'Hayling Billy' crosses the main road at Langstone on its way to Hayling Island in the latter days of the branch, 5 October 1963. The railwayman peering into the bunker - presumably the fireman - may well be attempting to clear an obstruction. The first coach will be noted to have observation windows indicating perhaps a pull-push set, although this type of working was not practised on the branch.

Chris Gammell C2751

STOKES BAY PIER: Stokes Bay was originally served by a branch having a triangular junction with the Gosport line just outside the latter station. The line, pier and ferry services commenced back in 1863 but were curtailed at the outbreak of WW1 never to resume. At the Gosport end, the triangular junction was retained for turning locomotives. Beyond this as far as the pier, the track was lifted although several of the bridges still remain. The pier itself was taken over by the Admiralty and used for torpedo testing. In this form it survived into the 1960s but has since been demolished. Traces of the railway heritage of the Gosport area, both its passenger and military lines - which were numerous, can still be seen decades later in the sinuous nature of various roads which had been originally laid out to avoid long gone railway lines.

Chris Gammell C756

FORT BROCKHURST: Drummond 0-6-0 No. 30327 arriving at Fort Brockhurst, once the junction for the Lee-on-the-Solent line, with the daily van train from Gosport. The line to Lee was served by a separate platform out of sight to the right of the main up platform. The working seen comprised just a single passenger brake van and despite the fact passengers services had been officially withdrawn from 8 June 1953, this service frequently carried passengers who were not railway staff. From 1935 through to 1957, Fort Brockhurst was a passing place on the single line between Fareham and Gosport, hence the signalman ready to pass the token to the crew. After this date the route all the way from Fareham was operated as one long section until the time of complete closure. The branch to Lee-on-the Solent had closed completely in 1935.

Brian Connell B20/2

FAREHAM: Train for the Meon Valley line. The Meon Valley route between Fareham and Alton operated until February 1955, some services continuing to or commencing from Gosport until that line had closed in 1953. Here M7 No. 30054 waits in the bay platform at Fareham, the site of which is now part of the station car park. It will leave shortly to call at Knowle, Wickham, Droxford, West Meon, Privett, East Tisted and Alton.

Brian Connell B24/3

SWANWICK: BR standard class 4, 2-6-0, No. 76064 with the 2.38 pm strawberries only train for York and Newcastle being loaded at Swanwick. In the 1950s it was still the practice for seasonal workings for this particular type of soft fruit; an interesting aspect being that the growers were often small operations who would deliver their produce by car, tractor and trailer, or even horse and cart to the station, collectively it made up sufficient for a train load.

Mike Walshaw 6434

BROOKWOOD NECROPOLIS: The Brookwood Necropolis Company had a very large cemetery adjacent to the station at Brookwood and, until it was destroyed by a German bomb, a private station at Waterloo where trains conveying coffins and mourners would start their journey to one of two stations within the Necropolis grounds. The service was not restored after WW2. When this view of the South station was taken in July 1955, the tracks were grass grown and the trains no longer ran. Even so there was still some activity with funeral parties now arriving by road and able to avail themselves of refreshments at the former station if required, accessible through the open doorway. This provision continued until 1967, long after the trains had ceased to run. The building was largely destroyed by fire on 22 September 1972.

Brian Connell B47/6

Left - SOUTHAMPTON TERMINUS: At the time the compiler of this book was commuting from Farnborough to Waterloo, his morning train (the 7.37 am from Farnborough) originated from Southampton Terminus at two minutes past six – thence stopping at all stations (eleven stops) to Farnborough after which it became more selective. Southampton Terminus was left off the map when the Bournemouth line was electrified in 1967 meaning that by the time of its closure in 1968, trains from the station served a dwindling number of destinations, not helped by the various line closures that had taken place. Only a decade earlier it had been the start and finish point for workings via Didcot, Cheltenham, Andover and the Wimborne line.

Roger Holmes R1839

Above - FAWLEY: An M7 class 0-4-4T ready to leave the branch terminus at Fawley with the 12.45 pm service for Southampton Central, 17 May 1958. Opened as late as 1926, this line saw more oil tank workings in and out of the refinery at Fawley, and traffic in connection with the military system at Marchwood, than ordinary passenger business. In 1952 an Aquila Flying Boat came to grief at nearby Calshot, the passengers from which were taken away from the area by an M7 and the regular three-coach set.

Hugh Davies 283B

ISLE of WIGHT: Left - The end of the line at Ventnor (Town) with O2 0-4-4T No. 33 'Bembridge' the subject of admiring (or is it even a cautionary?) gaze from two youthful observers.

Roger Holmes R1924

Top right - A platform view at Ventnor, seen from the buffer stops, 6 March 1955.

Norman Simmons N178A

Bottom right - Taken on the same day the station forecourt is decidedly deserted. A 'PLA' Passengers Luggage in Advance service was provided by the railway here in conjunction with the nationalised British Road Services. Under this arrangements suitcases, large bags and the like would be collected and transported to the holiday guest house / hotel so as to be ready for when the owner arrived.

Norman Simmons N178D

Opposite page - BEMBRIDGE: The most easterly station on the Island was at Bembridge where limited space meant a sector plate / turntable was provided instead of a head-shunt and full run-round loop. Here O2 0-4-4T No. 14 'Fishbourne' has just brought in the 1.10 pm train from the junction at Brading and will leave again at 1.32. The Bembridge line was one of several Island routes closed in the early 1950s, the others being the lines to Freshwater, Merstone, and Ventnor West.

Mike Walshaw 6015

Above - RYDE PIER HEAD: Until 1969, there was an alternative means of transport along Ryde Pier - the Ryde Pier Tramway, which had passed into the ownership of the Southern Railway in 1924. Seen is Drewry petrol railcar No. 1, purchased by the SR in 1927 and coupled to one of the two trailers built in 1936/37. Over its lifetime the tramway had been horse-worked, steam powered and electrified before turning over to petrol traction in November 1927.

Mike Walshaw 6173

CLAPHAM JUNCTION: Top left and opposite - These September 1954 views show the 12.25 pm Saturday only departure from Clapham junction to Kensington Olympia. Seen is the standard make-up for these services over many years; two former SECR 2-car sets, Nos. 513 and 514 with a third vehicle sandwiched between them. The stock was not pull-push fitted. Articulated sets Nos. 513 and 514 had previously worked the Sheppey Light railway until its closure in December 1950. The trains were provided primarily for the use of employees of the Post Office Savings Bank at Addison Road, Olympia and timed accordingly. Monday to Saturday there were two trains in each direction in the mornings; however at the end of the working day the timings varied with the days of the week; the Saturday working was at lunch-time, but the first departures from Kensington were at 4.6 pm on Fridays, 4.36 pm on Thursdays, and 5.6 pm Monday to Wednesday, with a second departure half-an-hour later in each case. This elaborate timetable was at the behest of the Post Office, but my memory of seeing the actual trains as we commuted past Clapham Junction tells me that they were little used.

Norman Simmons N458C & N458E

Bottom left - Clapham Junction A Signal Box occupied a strategic position straddling the tracks at the junction of the West London lines: from where this train of empty milk tanks is being hauled by M7 class 0-4-4T No. 30243. This box had a chequered history, suffering damage from a near miss by a German bomb, a fire shortly after this picture was taken, and a collapse in May 1965 when it had to be temporarily supported by the Nine Elms crane.

Norman Simmons N512C

MITCHAM JUNCTION: A single dome variant of the C2X 0-6-0 class, No. 32543 at Mitcham Junction with a pick-up freight from West Croydon. 27 February 1954.

Norman Simmons N106A

BRIXTON: W class 2-6-4T No. 31924 crossing the junction at Brixton on a cross– London (North / South) transfer freight on its way to Clapham Junction.

Norman Simmons N591C

SOUTH LAMBETH GOODS DEPOT: Strictly speaking these images should not be included, although the justification is simply that whilst definitely a Great Western outpost, geographically it was well inside Southern territory. The scenes were taken from a train heading towards Victoria and as might be imagined, access was only possible over Southern metals. Perhaps also not surprisingly the locomotives used were of the 0-6-0PT type, one member of the 57xx class being seen at work on 16 April 1955.

Norman Simmons N638D and N638E

CRYSTAL PALACE HIGH LEVEL: It was unusual for a terminal station in London, especially one as large as this, to be closed completely, but this was the fate of the former South Eastern station at Crystal Palace (High Level) seen here not long before services ceased from 20 September 1954. Seen is a 4-Sub unit, originally of three vehicles, but subsequently augmented with an additional vehicle, the profile of which is clearly different to the rest of the train.

Brian Connell B11/5

PETERSFIELD: A seemingly complex layout at Petersfield viewed from a convenient road overbridge just north of the station. Beyond the level crossing and signal box - both of which still exist today - is the main station sit. To the left is the branch platform used by trains for Midhurst. The site of the junction has nowadays long been obliterated by development and in consequence the double junction is of course no more. What remains is a simplified layout of just up and down main lines.

Norman Simmons N36D

PETWORTH: On what was almost the last day of passenger services to Midhurst, GPO mails are loaded at Petworth bound for Pulborough. The line closed from 6 February 1955.

Brian Connell B25/6

BARCOMBE MILLS: C2X 0-6-0 No. 32441 shunting the down siding at Barcombe Mills on a duty which, over two days, took it from Brighton to Lewes with freight: light engine to Newhaven: freight from Newhaven to Lewes and on to then Kingscote: back to Lewes with more freight: a diversion to Barcombe Mills (as seen here): return to Lewes: and finally light engine again to Brighton.

Norman Simmons 2309B

EAST GRINSTEAD: Throughout the 20 months of BR's enforced working of the line, to comply with the law over the closure of the Bluebell line, four trains a day operated in each direction, providing a roughly two-hour service seven days a week including Christmas Day. (One may wonder how much traffic was generated on the latter occasion?) Almost all the services were formed of a locomotive and single carriage, one such working seen on these pages at East Grinstead in 1958.

Norman Simmons 2814C and 2814B

NEWICK and CHAILEY: Even if they no longer hosted any traffic, most stations could claim to have goods facilities of some type, even if they were somewhat limited; witness here the goods shed at Newick and Chailey and decidedly on the small side. It was still operational, evidently mainly for coal, when this picture was taken.

Norman Simmons 2820C

NEWICK and CHAILEY: Possibly a unique event, certainly on the Southern, was the protest led by the redoubtable Miss Bessemer at the closure on 13 June 1955 of the line from Lewes to East Grinstead via Horsted Keynes. On 6 August 1956 British Railways reluctantly re-opened the line, K class 2-6-0 No. 32342 seen on the initial day of the reinstated service at Newick and Chailey in charge of the first northbound train.

Hugh Davies 72B

ABBOTSCLIFF: The track between Folkestone and Dover requires constant maintenance, consequently a set of sidings were provided for the use of the Civil Engineer, controlled by the signal box at Abbotscliff. Operationally, the box was only switched in at times of heavy traffic, which purpose was then to break up the section between Folkestone Junction and Dover, or when the Engineers were in operation. Here in 1958 the cabin has been switched into circuit, as H class 0-4-4T No. 31328 hauls a stopping service from Shornecliffe to Minster. The train also paused several times en-route to pick up staff along this stretch.

Norman Simmons 2496B

WARREN HALT: Between Folkestone Junction and Dover, at the foot of the cliffs, were a number of halts, mainly for railway staff use and associated with various signal cabins that were only occasionally switched in. In 1958 this unidentified 4-6-0 is taking a down train past Warren Halt, the exact position of which is also identified by milepost No. 72 on the platform.

Norman Simmons 2469A

FOLKESTONE HARBOUR: Half a dozen R1 class 0-6-6Ts survived at Folkestone Junction shed into the 1960s, mainly to work the boat trains on the Folkestone Harbour branch. Here two engines, one of which can be identified as No. 31047, take an up boat train over the water on the steep climb towards the junction.

David Lawrence 4532A

HEADCORN: The Kent and East Sussex platform at Headcorn with the single carriage forming the next departure for Tenterden at the platform. The O1 class engine is in the process of running round. January 1954.

Norman Simmons N105C

ROLVENDEN: The Colonel Stephens light railway atmosphere persisted right to the end of British Railway's ownership of the KESR route. An O1 class 0-6-0 and single coach confirming the rural idyll as it waits to enter Rolvenden with a train from Tenterden in the autumn of 1953. BR finally closed the line in 1954.

Norman Simmons N113A

SHARNAL STREET: The Kentish shore of the Thames Estuary was the home to a number of interesting branches each with a mysterious atmosphere of their own. Prominent among these were the railways of Hoo, at various times to Port Victoria, to Grain Crossing and to All Hallows. One of the intermediate stations was at Sharnal Street, seen here in 1958 with an H class 0-4-4T propelling a two-coach train towards All Hallows.

Norman Simmons 2805B

SHARNAL STREET: Although for much of its life most of the freight traffic on the branch was oil or its derivatives, there was still a significant amount of local mixed freight to the end. C class 0-6-0 No. 31579 is seen with both tank cars and other wagons, one of which is clearly the object of some interest from the resident railwayman.

Norman Simmons 2807A

RAMSGATE: L class 4-4-0 No. 31780 standing at the coaling stage at Ramsgate in 1957. At the time the newer traction depicted below was the latest in technology, yet time marches on and not just the steam engine seen here but the diesel and electric recorded in the lower view as well have all been consigned to history.

Norman Simmons 2337A

DOVER PRIORY: Electric, diesel and steam power at Dover Priory on 20 December 1960. At this Stage 1 of the Kent Coast Electrification Scheme had been completed, meaning it was the only the route via Faversham that had been electrified. The O1 shunting the yard was recorded as No. 31258.

Chris Gammell C1960

Top - NIGHT FERRY PASSENGER BRAKE VAN: Four-wheeled passenger brake van, No. S3, the last of a batch of three built at Ashford in June 1936 specifically for the Night Ferry service. All three remained on this duty until as late as 1960, when they lost their 'Night Ferry' branding and were repainted green (having previously been Wagons-Lits blue). This view shows the van very shortly after these changes but before the Westinghouse air brake equipment was removed.

David Lawrence 5486A

Right - CAR No. 16: It is difficult to imagine in these days that there would be sufficient demand to justify a Pullman Car service to and from the Kentish seaside resorts; yet here is Car. No. 16 at the end of the 'Thanet Belle' at Ramsgate, and looking very spruce in 1957.

Norman Simmons 2338C